A view of St. Peter's Church from the Tiber
St. Pierre vue d'une rive du Tibre
Eine Ansicht von St. Peter vom Tiberufer aus

ROME

ROM

A Book of Photographs by

R. S. MAGOWAN

With an Introduction by

RICHARD ALDINGTON

SPRING BOOKS · LONDON

First published 1960

Second impression 1963

Third impression 1964

Published by

SPRING BOOKS

WESTBOOK HOUSE • FULHAM BROADWAY

LONDON

© Paul Hamlyn Ltd. 1960

Printed in Czechoslovakia

T 1369

Contents

INTRODUCTION

BY RICHARD ALDINGTON

in English • 5   *en français* • 8   *auf deutsch* • 11

INDEX • 15

THE PLATES

TABLEAUX   BILDTEIL

ROME • 17

THE SIGHTS OF ROME • *Les Monuments de Rome* • *Roms Sehenswürdigkeiten* • 35

ROME AT LEISURE • *Rome en Flânant* • *Rom in seiner Freizeit* • 141

THE ARMS OF THE CITY OF ROME
LES ARMES DE LA CITE DE ROME
WAPPEN DER STADT ROM

Introduction

NOT so long ago visitors to Rome were far less numerous than they are now; but then, they stayed much longer, counting their visits not by weeks but by seasons. If comparative newcomers made the mistake of showing off very newly-acquired knowledge they were likely to be taken down by the question: 'Setting aside anything in museums, what would you say are the oldest works of man still extant in Rome?' It was pleasant to listen to the earnest discussions which followed from these six or eight weeks old archaeologists. The bronze Etruscan she-wolf was of course ruled out by being in a museum, and so too the magnificent Etruscan Apollo of Veii, but argument ran high about the comparative antiquity of the Niger Lapis in the Forum (supposed to mark the tomb of Romulus) and of 'the cippus' with its Latin inscription so archaic that few could read it even in the time of Cicero, and of the cloaca maxima which, according to Livy, was built for the Etruscan king, Tarquinius Priscus . . .

The solution to the riddle was as unanswerable as it was surprising to the victims. The oldest works of man still standing in Rome are neither Etruscan nor archaic Roman, but Egyptian — the obelisks. The oldest of these is in the piazza of San Giovanni in Laterano, was ordered from Egypt by Constantine and at last re-erected by his son Constantius II in A.D. 357 in the Circus Maximus. It carries the name of the 18th dynasty pharaoh, Tuthmosis IV, about 1400 B.C. The next most ancient stands in the Piazza del Popolo and bears the name of Rameses III (19th dynasty), said to have been ordered to Rome by Augustus to mark the final conquest of Egypt. In the last century the transport of one obelisk each to London, Paris and New York was the occasion for much newspaper self-laudation on the march of progress. Imperial Rome transported and set up nearly fifty such. Nobody seems to have reflected that the credit for these 'grotesque and unsightly monuments of Eastern superstition' belongs to the Egyptians who first thought of them and hewed them from quarries — in the later times, whether Roman or modern, it was entirely a matter of borrowed glory: borrowed without so much as a by-your-leave.

These forgotten discussions were really not so futile as might be supposed — there was more in them than a trick question and facts about obelisks. The originator, whoever he was, evidently meant to suggest by a kind of object lesson some truths about Rome. Old as it is, the City is younger than the great civilisations of the eastern Mediterranean. Moreover, vast as its influence has been, Rome was not so much a creative originator as a collector of cultural spoils, a great clearing-house of Mediterranean cultures and religions, art and learning. Its greatest service was the diffusion, however imperfect, of Hellenistic culture among the crude barbarians of the West. Even though Rome fell, enough was saved for civilisation to revive a millennium later. How immense was Rome's prestige may be seen from such facts as that until this century the proudest title of Europe was the name of 'Caesar', while the names of all our months are Roman, including of course 'Julius' and 'Augustus'. It was this prestige which awed the barbarian Alaric and induced him to let himself be bought off on one occasion for

5

less than the sack of the City. The same prestige enabled the Bishop of Rome to assert and maintain a supremacy over a great religious organisation which was started by Hebrews and systematised by Greeks, so that to Hobbes of Malmesbury the Papacy was 'the ghost of the old Roman Empire sitting crowned on the ruins thereof'.

A few buildings of ancient Rome have survived in more or less recognisable form, almost always because they were appropriated to Christian uses. Thus, in the Forum the well-known church of Saints Cosmas and Damian (A.D. 526) preserves the round temple built by Maxentius in 309 in memory of his son, Romulus. (Here again is Rome upon Rome. The name 'Romulus' sometimes misleads newcomers into thinking the building commemorates the legendary founder of Rome, or, more excusably, the boy Romulus nicknamed Augustulus, last of the Romans.) Again, the neighbouring San Lorenzo in Miranda has preserved the really beautiful temple of Antonius and Faustina. Between the Tiber and the church of Santa Maria in Cosmedin stand nineteen of the twenty original columns of the Round Temple, erroneously called Temple of Vesta — converted into a church in the Middle Ages. The neighbouring Doric temple (very doubtfully of Fortuna Virilis) was preserved first as Santa Maria Gradellis, and in the 15th century as Santa Maria Egizaca, who naturally became the patron of the courtesans who thronged the quarter at that time. The most spectacular of these comparatively unharmed structures is the Pantheon, robbed indeed of its gold and bronze and statues of the gods, but still structurally intact.

Rome is like a geological formation of stratum upon stratum of civilisations, the creation, destruction, re-creation, re-making of a hundred generations. Like natural rock layers, the strata of Rome are folded, crumpled, distorted, obliterated, with the newer Romes made of fragments of the old as the detritus of millennia form the new sedimentary rocks.

Yet Rome, though a city of the mighty dead, is not a dead city, standing desolate like Petra or Baalbek, or disinterred like Pompeii or Timgad. It is the capital of a modern State, housing or failing to house a million of the liveliest people in Europe. A few areas are indeed kept sacred to the past, old buildings protected, but the old quarters are pulled down and reconstructed, new quarters built, and everywhere what used to be called the picturesque is destroyed. A century ago the wild plants growing on the Colosseum were so numerous and interesting that a botanist wrote a special book about them — the hideous neatness of the enlightened municipality has swept all away. Time was when at night as you stood at the top of the Scala di Spagna you could hear the rushing of Rome's fountains. Inevitably a newer, more crowded Rome has been superimposed on the Rome some of us knew only yesterday.

Let us take the famous walk from the end of the Via Sistina to the Pincian terrace, and stand for a moment to look down into the Piazza di Spagna, so-named for no better reason than the Spanish embassy was in it. The flower-sellers at the foot of the great flight of steps almost hide Bernini's curious fountain in the shape of a boat — to explain which everyone has a different story. Just across the way Byron lived, and in the house to our left at the side of the steps Keats died. Among the beauties of Rome we must rank noble flights of steps, and the Scala di Spagna is one of the finest — a curious misnomer, for they were paid for by an 18th century French diplomat to form a worthy approach to the Trinità dei Monti, the church of the French nuns of the Sacré Cœur. Mendelssohn used to go to their services to listen to the unseen singers, and even composed music for them.

In early spring, or late winter, the mimosas underneath the supporting wall of the walk were fragrant. A little farther on, opposite the entrance to the Villa Medici, is one of the most frequently sketched scenes of Rome — the fountain-jet rising and falling into the shapely stone *vasque* under the clipped ilex trees, with the glimpse of St Peter's dome in the background. Whence came the great stone basin of the fountain? Perhaps from the gardens of Lucullus which once covered these heights.

And so we come to the Pincian terrace. Certainly it would be untrue to say that this is the finest view of Rome, but one cannot be always going as far as the Aventine or the Janiculum, still less climbing up the tower of the Capitol or the dome of St Peter's — true as it is that the high views of Rome are the best. The Janiculum

6

is too far off, and the Aventine is now becoming so built over that soon the only view will be the famous one through the keyhole to the entrance of the Villa of the Knights of Malta. No, the Pincian terrace is the most accessible point of survey, and indeed it is there that most people take their first impressions and last farewells of the City. It is surprising how much of Rome can be seen from so comparatively low a height, a great semicircle from Monte Mario to the Victor Emmanuel monument, with St Peter's dome superbly set against the horizon, gold as a Jubilee or scarlet as the Albigensian crusade.

Introduction

Il n'y a pas si longtemps, les visiteurs étaient beaucoup moins nombreux à Rome, mais ils y faisaient de bien plus longs séjours, comptant non par semaines mais par saisons. Si de relatifs néophytes commettaient l'erreur d'étaler des connaissances un peu trop fraîchement acquises, ils ne manquaient pas de se voir poser la question: «Mises à part les collections des musées, quels sont à votre avis les plus anciens monuments de Rome?» Il était amusant d'entendre les graves discussions qui s'engageaient entre ces archéologues de six ou huit semaines. La louve étrusque était naturellement écartée, comme faisant partie d'un musée, de même que le magnifique Apollon étrusque de Veii, mais on s'interrogeait sur l'âge relatif de la pierre noire du Forum qui marque, dit-on, l'endroit où fut enterré Romulus et du «cippus» avec son inscription latine si archaïque que peu de gens pouvaient la comprendre même au temps de Cicéron, ou la «cloaca maxima» qui, selon Tite-Live, fut construite pour le roi d'Etrurie . . .

La solution était aussi imprévisible que surprenante pour les victimes. Les plus anciens monuments de Rome ne sont ni étrusques, ni romains, mais égyptiens; ce sont les obélisques. Le plus ancien de tous se trouve sur la place St Jean-de-Latran. Commandé par Constantin, il fut érigé à Rome, au Circus Maximus, par son fils Constantin II en 357. Il porte le nom de la 18ème dynastie des pharaons, Tuthmosis IV (1400 ans av. J. C.). Ensuite, le plus ancien est l'obélisque de la piazza del Popolo, portant le nom de Ramsès II (19ème dynastie), qui aurait été commandé par Auguste pour commémorer la conquête définitive de l'Egypte. Au siècle dernier, se transport d'un obélisque à Londres, à Paris et à New York fut l'occasion dans la presse de grandes exclamations sur les merveilles du progrès. La Rome impériale en transporta et en érigea près de cinquante. Personne ne semble avoir remarqué que le mérite de ces «grotesques et inconvenants monuments de la superstition orientale» revient aux Egyptiens, qui en eurent les premiers l'idée et les taillèrent dans la pierre de leurs carrières. Plus tard, que ce soit à Rome ou dans les temps modernes, la gloire leur en fut empruntée, sans même qu'on songe à leur en faire crédit.

Ces discussions d'alors n'étaient en vérité pas si futiles qu'on pourrait le supposer, elles contenaient plus qu'une devinette et quelques données sur les obélisques. L'auteur voulait certainement par une sorte de leçon de choses, mettre en relief quelques vérités sur Rome. Si ancienne qu'elle soit, la ville l'est moins que les grandes civilisations de la Méditerranée orientale. De plus, si vaste qu'ait été son influence, Rome n'a pas été tellement créatrice; elle a surtout collectionné les grandes œuvres de la civilisation, elle fut un carrefour des cultures, des religions, de l'art et des sciences de tout le monde méditerranéen. Le plus grand service qu'elle rendit, fut de diffuser, si imparfaitement que ce soit, la culture hellénique parmi les grossiers barbares de l'Occident. Et à sa chute, elle avait sauvé assez pour que la civilisation revive un millénaire plus tard. On peut mesurer l'immensité du prestige de Rome au fait, par exemple, que jusqu'à ce siècle, le titre le plus fier de l'Europe était le nom de César, tandis que nos mois portent des noms romains, y compris, naturellement, «Julius» et «Augustus».

C'est ce prestige qui effraya le barbare Alaric et une fois le conduisit à se laisser acheter pour moins que le sac de la ville. Ce même prestige permit à l'évêque de Rome d'affirmer et de maintenir son autorité sur une grande organisation religieuse commencée par les Hébreux et systématisée par les Grecs, de sorte que jusqu'à Hobbes, la Papauté fut le «fantôme du vieil Empire romain assis couronné sur les ruines de Rome».

Quelques édifices de la Rome antique ont survécu sous une forme plus ou moins identifiable, presque toujours parce qu'ils furent affectés au culte chrétien. Ainsi, au Forum, la fameuse église Sts Côme et Damien (526) préserve le temple circulaire par Maxence en 309 en mémoire de son fils Romulus (là encore, Rome recouvre Rome. Le nom de Romulus induit quelquefois les profanes à croire qu'il s'agit du légendaire fondateur de Rome ou, de façon moins inexcusable, le petit Romulus surnommé Augustulus, le dernier des Romains). Non loin de là, San Lorenzo in Miranda a préservé le très beau temple d'Antonin et Faustine. Entre le Tibre et l'église Santa Maria-in-Cosmedin, on retrouve dix-neuf des vingt colonnes du temple circulaire, appelé à tort temple de Vesta, transformé en église pendant le moyen âge. Le temple dorique dit de la Fortune virile devint l'église Santa Maria Gradellis et au XVème siècle Santa Maria Egizaca, devenue naturellement la patronne des courtisans qui vivaient nombreux dans le quartier à l'époque. Le plus spectaculaire de ces édifices presque intacts et le Panthéon, qui a été dépouillé à la vérité de ses ors, de ses bronzes et des statues des dieux, mais dont l'intérieur est resté tel quel.

Rome est comme une coupe géologique composée de couches de civilisations superposées, création, destruction, recréation, refonte de centaines de générations successives. Comme des couches de roches naturelles, les «strata» de Rome sont plissés, érodées, déformées, détruites, et les Romes nouvelles s'incorporent aux fragments des anciennes comme les dépôts des siècles s'agglomèrent pour former de nouveaux sédiments.

Pourtant Rome, ville d'ombres géantes, n'est pas une ville morte, désolée comme Pétra ou Baalbek, ou exhumée comme Pompéï ou Timgad. C'est la capitale d'un Etat moderne, qui abrite (ou n'abrite pas) un million d'hommes parmi les plus vivants d'Europe. Quelques parties de la ville sont consacrées au passé, quelques monuments sont protégés, mais de vieux quartiers sont abattus et reconstruits, de nouveaux quartiers s'élèvent et partout ce que l'on avait coutume d'appeler le pittoresque disparaît. Il y a un siècle, les plantes sauvages qui poussaient au Colisée étaient si abondantes et si intéressantes qu'un botaniste put écrite un livre à leur sujet. Une municipalité éclairée y a mis bon ordre. Il fut un temps où du haut des escaliers de la place d'Espagne, la nuit, vous pouviez entendre le murmure des fontaines de Rome. Inévitablement, une Rome plus moderne, plus peuplée, s'est surimposée à la Rome que nous fûmes quelques-uns à connaître naguère.

Refaisons la fameuse promenade depuis la via Sistina jusqu'à la terrasse du Pincio et arrêtons-nous un moment pour jeter un regard sur la place d'Espagne, qui doit son nom au simple fait que l'ambassade d'Espagne y était autrefois située. Les marchands de fleurs au pied du grand escalier cachent presque la curieuse fontaine du Bernin, en forme de bâteau, dont chacun donne une interprétation différente. C'est juste en face qu'habitait Byron et c'est dans la maison située à gauche de l'escalier que Keats mourut. Parmi les beautés de Rome, il faut compter ses nobles escalier et celui-ci est l'un des plus beaux. Son nom est mal choisi, car il fut commandé par un diplomate français du XVIIIème siècle pour fournir une belle voie d'accès à Trinità dei Monti, l'église des sœurs françaises du Sacré Cœur. Mendelssohn se rendait à leurs offices pour y écouter les chanteurs invisibles, et il leur composa même de la musique.

Au début du printemps, ou vers la fin de l'hiver, les mimosas au pied du mur de l'allée embaumaient. Un peu plus loin, en face de l'entrée de la villa Medicis, on découvre l'une des scènes les plus fréquemment peintes de Rome, le jet d'eau qui s'élève et retombe dans la jolie vasque sous les yeuses taillées, et la vue sur le dôme de St Pierre au loin. D'où est venue la pierre du bassin de la fontaine? Peut-être des jardins de Luculus qui s'étendaient autrefois sur ces hauteurs.

Et nous voici arrivés sur la terrasse du Pincio. Il serait faux de dire que c'est la plus belle vue de Rome, mais on ne peut toujours aller jusque sur l'Aventin ou sur le Janicule, encore moins monter sur la tour du Capitole ou sur le dôme de St Pierre, pour vrai qu'il soit que les plus hauts points sont ceux d'où l'on découvre Rome le mieux. Le Janicule est trop loin, et l'Aventin est maintenant si construit que bientôt la seule vue sera celle, fameuse, du trou de la serrure d'entrée de la villa des Chevaliers de l'Ordre de Malte. Non, la terrasse du Pincio est le point de vue le plus accessible, et c'est là que la plupart des visiteurs forment leurs premières impressions de Rome et viennent faire leurs derniers adieux. On est surpris de découvrir quelle large part de la ville on embrasse d'un promontoire relativement peu élevé, un grand demi-cercle de Monte Mario au monument de Victor Emmanuel, avec le dôme de St Pierre superbement détaché à l'horizon, doré comme un jubilé ou écarlate comme la croisade des Albigeois.

Einleitung

VOR nicht allzu langer Zeit war die Zahl der Besucher Roms noch weit geringer als heute; doch damals blieben sie länger, sie zählten ihren Aufenthalt nicht nach Wochen, sondern nach Jahreszeiten. Wenn Neuankömmlinge den Fehler begingen, mit frischerworbenen Kenntnissen hervorzutreten, dann wurde ihre Hochstimmung gern mit der Frage gedämpft: „Und wenn wir einmal absehen von den Gegenständen in den Museen: was würden Sie dann in Rom als die ältesten Werke von Menschenhand betrachten?" Es war vergnüglich, den ersten Erörterungen zuzuhören, die daraufhin unter diesen sechs oder acht Wochen alten Archäologen begannen. Die Kapitolinische Wölfin fiel natürlich aus, da sie sich in einem Museum befand, ebenso der herrliche etruskische Apollo von Veji; aber heiß wogte der Kampf um das vergleichbare Alter des Lapis niger im Forum (von dem man glaubte, er bezeichne das Grab des Romulus) — des Cippus mit seiner so altertümlichen lateinischen Inschrift, daß selbst zu Zeiten des Cicero nur wenige sie lesen konnten — und der Cloaca maxima, die nach Livius für den Etruskerkönig Tarquinius Priscus erbaut wurde ...

Die Lösung des Rätsels war so unwiderlegbar wie verblüffend für die Opfer: Die ältesten in Rom erhaltenen Werke von Menschenhand sind weder etruskischen noch altrömischen, sondern ägyptischen Ursprungs — die Obelisken. Der älteste wiederum unter ihnen steht auf der Piazza S. Giovanni in Laterano, wurde von Konstantin aus Ägypten herbeigeschafft und schließlich von seinem Sohn Constantius II, 357 n. Chr. im Circus Maximus neu aufgestellt. Er trägt den Namen eines Pharao der 18. Dynastie, Thutmosis' IV., um 1400 v. Chr. Der nächstälteste steht auf der Piazza del Popolo, unter dem Namen Ramses' III. (19. Dynastie); er wurde angeblich zum Zeichen der endgültigen Unterwerfung Ägyptens von Augustus nach Rom gebracht. Im vergangenen Jahrhundert nahm die Presse den Transport je eines Obelisken nach London, Paris und New York zum Anlaß großer Lobeserhebungen auf den unaufhaltsamen technischen Fortschritt. Das kaiserliche Rom hat fast fünfzig solcher Obelisken abtransportiert und wieder aufgestellt. Niemand scheint darüber nachgedacht zu haben, daß das Verdienst an diesen „grotesken und unansehnlichen Monumenten östlichen Aberglaubens" den Ägyptern zukommt, die sie aufbrachten und aus Steinbrüchen schlugen, — später, ob zu Zeiten des alten Rom oder in der Moderne, war es ein geborgter Glanz, geborgt ohne auch nur die Andeutung einer Bitte um Erlaubnis.

Diese längst vergangenen Erörterungen waren in Wirklichkeit nicht ganz so sinnlos, wie es scheinen könnte: es ging darin um mehr als um eine Trickfrage und um Obelisken. Der sie einführte, wer immer es war, wollte offenbar mit einer Art von Anschauungsunterricht einige Wahrheiten über Rom aufzeigen. So alt sie ist, die Stadt ist jünger als die großen Zivilisationen des östlichen Mittelmeergebiets. Darüber hinaus war Rom, dessen Einfluß ungeheuer weit reichte, nicht so sehr ursprünglich und schöpferisch tätig; seine Stärke lag vielmehr im Zusammentragen kulturellen Beuteguts, es war ein großer Umschlagplatz von Kulturen und Religionen, Kunst und Wissen des Mittelmeerraums. Sein bedeutendstes Verdienst war die — allerdings unvollkommene — Verbreitung hellenistischer Kultur unter den Barbaren des Westens. Wenn Rom auch unterging, so blieb doch genügend erhalten, um die Zivilisation ein Jahrtausend später wiederaufleben zu lassen. Wie unermeßlich Roms Prestige war, geht zum Beispiel daraus hervor, daß bis in unser Jahrhundert hinein der stolzeste Titel Europas dem Namen „Caesar" nachgebildet war; und tragen nicht all unsere Monate römische Bezeichnungen, einschließlich natürlich der Namen „Julius" und „Augustus"? Es war dieser Ruhm, der seinen Eindruck auf den Barbaren Alarich nicht verfehlte und ihn in einem Fall bewog, sich auch ohne Plünderung Roms zufriedenzugeben. Und das gleiche Prestige ermöglichte es dem Bischof von Rom, die Oberhoheit über eine große Religionsgemeinschaft geltend zu machen und zu behaupten, die von Hebräern gegründet und von Griechen ausgebaut worden war, — so daß das Papsttum dem Philosophen Thomas Hobbes vorkam wie „der Geist des alten römischen Kaiserreichs, der über dessen Ruinen thront".

Einige Bauten des alten Rom sind in mehr oder weniger erkennbarer Form erhalten geblieben, fast durchweg weil sie in den Gebrauch des Christentums übergingen. So ist in die bekannte Kirche der Heiligen Kosmas und Damian (526 n. Chr.) auf dem Forum der Rundtempel einbezogen, den Maxentius 309 zum Gedächtnis seines Sohnes Romulus bauen ließ. (Auch hier wieder verschmelzen verschiedene Epochen Roms miteinander. Der Name Romulus verleitet Neuankömmlinge manchmal zu der Ansicht, das Gebäude erinnere an den sagenhaften Gründer der Stadt oder — entschuldbarer — an den Knaben Romulus mit dem Beinamen Augustulus, den letzten weströmischen Kaiser.) Der nahegelegenen Kirche S. Lorenzo in Miranda hinwiederum verdanken wir den Fortbestand des wirklich herrlichen Tempels von Antoninus und Faustina. Zwischen dem Tiber und der Kirche S. Maria in Cosmedin stehen neunzehn der zwanzig Originalsäulen des einstigen Rundtempels, fälschlicherweise Tempel der Vesta genannt — im Mittelalter in eine Kirche umgewandelt. Der benachbarte dorische Tempel (sehr ungewiß, ob der Fortuna Virilis geweiht) wurde zunächst zur Kirche S. Maria Gradellis, im 15. Jahrhundert umbenannt in S. Maria Egizaca (Maria von Ägypten), die natürlich als Patronin der Freudenmädchen dienen mußte, welche zur damaligen Zeit jenes Stadtviertel bevölkerten. Das großartigste dieser verhältnismäßig unbeschädigten Bauwerke ist das Pantheon, das zwar Gold und Bronze und die Statuen der Götter einbüßte, aber in der Struktur unverändert blieb.

Rom gleicht einer geologischen Formation übereinandergelagerter Zivilisationen, an der sich Aufstieg, Untergang und abermalige Erneuerung unzähliger Generationen ablesen lassen. Wie natürliche Gesteinsschichten zeigen die Entwicklungsstadien Roms Falten und Verschiebungen, Schrumpfungen, Zerstörung und Verwandlung; das jeweilige neue Rom erstand aus den Trümmern des alten, wie das Geröll von Jahrtausenden neues Sedimentgestein bildet.

Aber Rom — die Stadt, in welcher der Tod so schrecklich seine Macht erwiesen hat — ist keine tote Stadt, verlassen und verwüstet wie Petra oder Baalbek, ausgegraben wie Pompeji oder Timgad. Es ist die Hauptstadt eines modernen Staates und bietet (oder bietet auch nicht) einer Million der springlebendigsten Einwohner Europas Obdach. Wohl sind einige wenige Gebiete dem Gedächtnis der Vergangenheit vorbehalten, antike Bauten geschützt, doch die alten Viertel sind niedergerissen und wieder aufgebaut, neue Viertel erstanden, und der „pittoreske" Charakter ist verschwunden. Vor einem Jahrhundert noch war der Pflanzenwuchs im Kolosseum so reichhaltig und interessant, daß ein Botaniker ein eigenes Buch darüber schrieb, aber der unerbittliche Ordnungsdrang einer aufgeklärten Stadtverwaltung hat alles hinweggefegt. Die Zeiten sind vergangen, da man nachts auf den obersten Stufen der Spanischen Treppe das Rauschen und Plätschern der Brunnen Roms hören konnte. Eine neue, noch überfülltere Stadt hat sich zwangsläufig über das alte Rom gebreitet, das einige von uns vor gar nicht langer Zeit noch gekannt haben.

Gehen wir den berühmten Weg vom Ende der Via Sistina auf die Terasse des Monte Pincio und bleiben wir einen Augenblick stehen, um auf die Piazza di Spagna hinunterzusehen, die ihren Namen lediglich der Tatsache verdankt, daß sich dort die Spanische Botschaft befand. Die Blumenverkäufer am Fuß der großangelegten Treppe verbergen fast Berninis seltsamen bootförmigen Brunnen — zu dessen Erklärung jedermann eine andere Geschichte erzählt. Gerade gegenüber lebte Byron, und in dem Haus zur Linken, auf der Seite der Treppe, starb

Keats. Elegante Treppenfluchten gehören zu den Schönheiten Roms, und die Spanische Treppe ist eine der prachtvollsten, — eine seltsame Fehlbezeichnung, denn die Kosten dafür trug ein französischer Diplomat des 18. Jahrhunderts, der einen würdigen Aufgang zur Kirche Trinità dei Monti geschaffen sehen wollte, der Kirche der französischen Ordensfrauen von Sacré-Cœur. Mendelssohn pflegte ihren Gottesdiensten beizuwohnen, um dem Gesang des unsichtbaren Chors zu lauschen, und komponierte sogar einiges für sie.

In den ersten Frühlingstagen, oder im späten Winter, beginnen die Mimosen unterhalb der Schutzmauer des Weges zu duften. Etwas weiter, gegenüber dem Eingang zur Villa Medici, bietet sich eine der in Skizzen und Zeichnungen mit Vorliebe dargestellten Szenen Roms: der aufsteigende Strahl des Springbrunnens, wieder herabstürzend in das ebenmäßige Becken unter den gestutzten Stechpalmensträuchern, im Hintergrund fern die Kuppel von St. Peter. Woher dieses große, steinerne Becken des Brunnens stammt? Vielleicht aus den Gärten des Lucullus, die sich einst über diese Anhöhen breiteten.

Und so kommen wir zur Terrasse des Monte Pincio. Es wäre zweifellos unrichtig, wollte man sagen, dies sei die schönste Ansicht von Rom, aber man kann nicht immer bis zum Aventin oder zum Janiculum vordringen und schon gar nicht auf den Turm des Kapitols oder die Kuppel von St. Peter steigen — so sehr es zutrifft, daß Rom aus luftiger Höhe den besten Anblick bietet. Doch der Hügel des Janiculum liegt zu weit ab, und der Aventin wird allmählich so zugebaut, daß bald die einzige Aussicht, die bleibt, der berühmte Blick durchs Schlüsselloch sein wird. Nein, die Terrasse des Monte Pincio gewährt den am leichtesten zugänglichen Überblick, und tatsächlich nehmen dort die meisten Menschen ihre ersten Eindrücke und die letzten Grüße der Stadt entgegen. Es ist erstaunlich, wie viel man von dieser verhältnismäßig niedrigen Anhöhe aus von Rom sehen kann: das Halbrund vom Monte Mario bis zum Denkmal Viktor Emmanuels II., am Horizont die strahlende, herrliche Kuppel von St. Peter.

THE ARMS OF THE VATICAN
LES ARMES DU VATICAN
WAPPEN DES VATIKANS

Index

Agnese in Agone, S., 53
Angel by Bernini, 60
Appian Way, 108—9
Arch of Augustus, 61
Arch of Constantine, 71
Arch of Janus Quadrifons, 69
Arch of Septimus Severus, 63—4
Arch of Titus, 70
Aurelian Wall, 93, 109

Basilica of Constantine, 95
Basilica Julia, 66
Byron, statue of, 124

Capitol, 34, 73—6
Capitoline Square, 72
Caracalla, Baths of, 111
Carlo ai Catinari, S., 128
Casino of Pius IV, 81
Colonnades in St. Peter's Square, 43—4,
    113
Colosseum (Flavian Amphitheatre),
    56—8, 110
Croce in Gerusalemme, S., 103

Discobolus, 159
Discori, 74—5

Firdousi, statue of, 124
Fontana del Fiumi, 53, 147
Fontana di Trevi, 48
Forum Romanum, 61, 63—5, 88—9,
    145
Fountain of the Republic, 145
Fountain of the Triton, 50

Galleria Borghese, 129
Garibaldi Monument, 123
Giovanni in Laterano, S., 96—7
Giovanni e Paolo, SS., 99
Gregorio Magno, S., 106

House of the Vestal Virgins, 95

Janiculum Promenade, 123, 125, 127

Maderna's fountain, 45
Marble Stadium (Campo della Farne-
    sina), 90
Marcus Aurelius, statue of, 72
Maria di Loreto, S., 35, 86
Maria in Aracoeli, S., 102
Maria in Cosmedin, S., 68
Maria in Trastevere, S., 101
Martina e Luca, SS., 64, 66
Moses, Michelangelo's, 121

Neptune Fountain, 46
Nome di Maria, SS., 35, 86—7

Obelisks, 18, 51—4
Ostia Beach, 143

Palatine, 91
Palazzo dei Senatori, 72—6
Pantheon, 18, 51
Paolo fuori le Mura, S., 98, 100, 120
Piazza Barberini, 50
Piazza Cairoli, 128
Piazza del Popolo, 47, 54
Piazza della Minerva, 51
Piazza della Rotonda, 47
Piazza di S. Giovanni in Laterano, 52,
    97
Piazza di Spagna, 37
Piazza Navona, 46, 53
Piazzale Brasile, 132
Pietro in Vincoli, S., 121
Pincio Hill, 126
Ponte Fabricio, 139
Porta Maggiore, 92
Porta Pia, 83
Porta S. Sebastiano, 93, 106—7
Protestant Cemetery, 80
Pyramid of Caius Cestius, 80

St. Peter's Church, 39, 41—3, 90,
    114—17, 160

St. Peter's Square, 43—5, 52, 113—14,
    150
S. Angelo, Bridge and Castle of, 18, 38,
    60
SS. Apostoli, 119
Spanish Steps, 37
Station Termini, 138
Swiss Guard, 117

Temple of Aesculapius, 79
Temple of Antoninus and Faustina, 61
Temple of Castor and Pollux, 66
'Temple of Fortuna Virilis', 77
Temple of Saturn, 64—5
Temple of Vespasian, 64—5
'Temple of Vesta', 68—9
Theatre of Marcellus, 59, 112
Tiber, 42, 138—142
Tiber Island, 139
Tivoli, 49
Tomb of Caecilia Metella, 109
Trajan's Column, 35, 84—7
Trajan's Forum, 62
Trastevere Quarter, 134
Trinità dei Monti, SS., 37

Vatican, 117
Vatican Gardens, 41, 81, 129
Vatican Museums, 82
Vatican Picture Gallery, 104—5
Venus staute, 159
Via Amba Aradam, 136—7
Via Cavour, 94
Via del Corso, 55
Via della Conciliazione, 42
Via Venti Settembre, 83
Villa Borghese, 78—9, 146
Villa d'Este, 49
Villa Medici, 40
Victor Emmanuel II Monument, 21,
    35—6, 122
Vitale, S., 118

COLOUR PLATES

A view of St. Peter's Church from the
    Tiber, *frontispiece*
St. Pierre vue d'une rive du Tibre,
    frontispice
Eine Ansicht von St. Peter vom Tiber-
    ufer aus, *Frontispiz*

The Colosseum at night, *facing p. 16*
Le Colisée au soir, *en regard de la page 16*
Das Kolosseum abends, *gegenüber der
    Seite 16*

Fashion in Rome, *facing p. 17*
Elégance à Rome, *en regard de la page 17*
Eleganz in Rom, *gegenüber der Seite 17*

The Colosseum at night
Le Colisée au soir
Das Kolosseum abends

Fashion in Rome
Elégance à Rome
Eleganz in Rom

London has its buses . . .

Paris has its taxis . . .

. . . and

ROME

has its scooters, the
volatile scooters which express the modern
Roman's penchant for fast and lively travel

Londres a ses bus . . .
Paris a ses taxis . . .
. . . et ROME a ses scooters, ces effervescents
petits véhicules qui traduisent le goût du Romain
moderne pour la vitesse et le mouvement

London hat seine Busse . . .
Paris hat seine Taxis . . .
. . . und ROM hat seine Motorroller, diese wen-
digen Fahrzeuge, welche die Vorliebe des modernen Römers für schnelle und lebhafte Fahrweise
verkörpern

The classic-faced Pantheon looks on without surprise as two young priests scoot across the Piazza della Rotonda: a further touch of the incongruous is provided by the obelisk from ancient Egypt

Le Panthéon au fronton classique observe sans surprise deux prêtres débouchant en scooter sur la place de la Rotonde; l'Obélisque, vestige de l'ancienne Egypte, ajoute à l'incongru de la scène

Die klassische Fassade des Pantheon zeigt kein Erstaunen, als zwei junge Geistliche mit dem Motorroller über die Piazza della Rotonda fahren; ein weiterer Gegensatz: der altägyptische Obelisk

Scooter on the S. Angelo Bridge
Scooter sur le pont St Ange
Motorroller auf der Engelsbrücke

Scooters everywhere in Rome . . .
Scooters partout . . .
Motorroller allüberall in Rom . . .

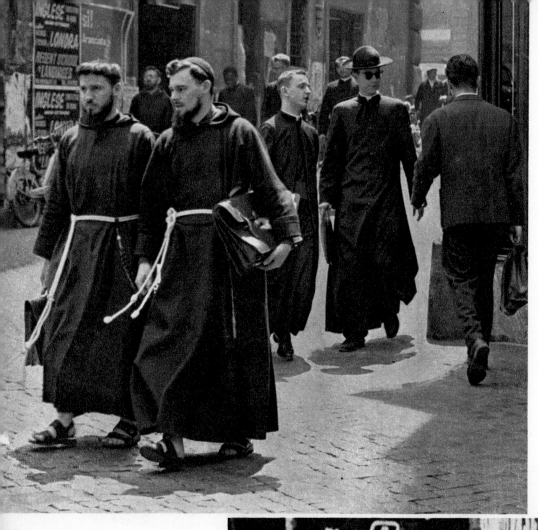

... but there are still those who use their legs
... mais il reste encore des piétons
... aber es gibt auch noch Fußgänger

While Rome burns in the sun, a marble god reclines...
Tandis que Rome se consume au soleil, un Dieu de marbre se repose...
Während Rom in der Sonnenglut flimmert, ruht auch der marmorne Gott entspannt...

... and some citizens sleep
... et quelques citoyens s'assoupissent
... und so mancher der Einwohner schläft

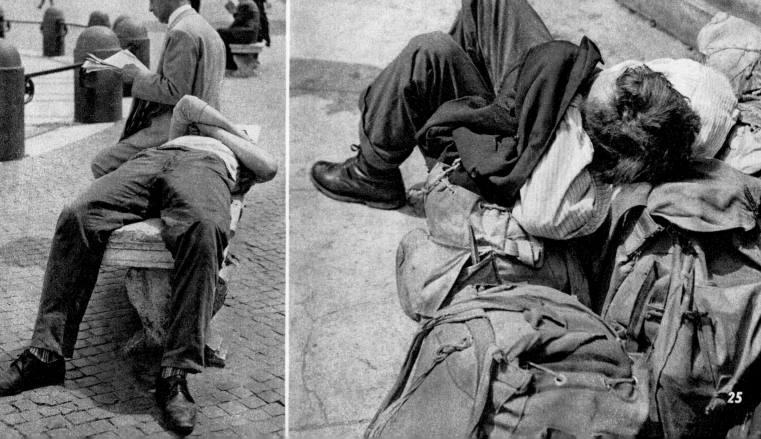

A city has many faces . . .
Une ville a de nombreux visages . . .
Eine Stadt hat viele Gesichter . . .

. . . some haughty
. . . les uns hautains
. . . abweisende

. . . some disgruntled
. . . ou maussades
. . . mürrische

. . . some puzzled
. . . les autres perplexes
. . . grüblerische

... some apprehensive: will it rain?
... d'autres appréhensifs: Pleuvra-t-il?
... besorgte: Wird es regnen?

Yes, it will!
Oui!
Ja, es wird!

But let us think of Rome as a city blessed by the sun . . .
Mais imaginons plutôt Rome comme une ville inondée de soleil . . .
Aber denken wir an Rom als die Stadt der ewigen Sonne. . .

. . . and especially on washing day
. . . surtout par un jour de lessive
. . . vor allem am Waschtag

The tourist season in full swing . . .
En pleine saison de tourisme . . .
Breit fließt der Touristenstrom . . .

. . . mamma mia, these tourists!
. . . mamma mia, ces touristes!
. . . mamma mia, diese Touristen!

So much to see in Rome: sometimes it is a problem where to go next
Il y a tant à voir à Rome: parfois la question est de savoir où l'on ira ensuite
Es gibt so viel zu sehen in Rom, manchmal wird die Reihenfolge zum Problem

THE SIGHTS OF
ROME

Not to everybody's taste: the grandiose, neo-classical monument to Victor Emmanuel II, begun in 1885 and dedicated in 1911
Pas au goût de tout le monde: le grandiose monument néo-classique à Victor-Emmanuel II, commencé en 1885, achevé en 1911
Nicht jedermanns Geschmack: das grandiose, neoklassizistische Denkmal Viktor Emmanuels II., 1885 begonnen, 1911 eingeweiht

The much-loved Spanish Steps, which link the Piazza di Spagna to the Trinità dei Monti church.
D'Annunzio the poet said these steps were designed 'for leisure and amorous couples'

Les célèbres escaliers d'Espagne qui relient la place d'Espagne à l'église Trinité-des-Monts. Le poète
d'Annunzio a écrit que ces marches sont dédiées « au loisir et aux amoureux »

Die beliebte Spanische Treppe, Verbindung der Piazza di Spagna mit der Kirche Trinità dei Monti.
Der Dichter d'Annunzio sagte, diese Treppe sei „zur Muße und für Liebespaare" geschaffen

The Bridge and Castle of S. Angelo, impressively evocative of Rome's past: the Castle was built by Hadrian as a mausoleum for himself and his successors, and later became the citadel of the Popes

Le pont et le château Saint-Ange évoquent la Rome antique: le château a été construit par Hadrien pour servir de mausolée à lui-même et à ses successeurs; il devint plus tard la citadelle des papes

In Engelsbrücke und Engelsburg ersteht eindrucksvoll Roms Vergangenheit: Die Burg wurde als Mausoleum für Kaiser Hadrian und seine Nachfolger erbaut; später war sie Stützpunkt und Zufluchtsort der Päpste

Majestic St Peter's dominating the view for miles around is the dome of the largest and most splendid church in Christendom

La majestueuse basilique St Pierre: à des kilomètres de distance, on reconnaît le dôme de la plus grande et de la plus belle église de la Chrétienté

Der majestätische Bau von St. Peter: kilometerweit in die Runde beherrscht die Kuppel dieser größten und prächtigsten Kirche der Christenheit den Blick

The great dome of St. Peter's, outward and visible symbol of the Catholic Church, viewed from the gardens of the Vatican
Le grand dôme de St Pierre, symbole visible de l'Eglise catholique, vu des jardins du Vatican
Blick aus den päpstlichen Gärten auf die Kuppel von St. Peter, äußeres und sichtbares Wahrzeichen der katholischen Kirche

A jewel of Renaissance architecture: the Villa Medici, built in 1544, and since 1803 the home of the French Academy in Rome
Un joyau de l'architecture de la Renaissance : la villa Médicis, construite en 1544, depuis 1803 la propriété de l'Académie française
Ein Juwel der Renaissance-Architektur: die Villa Medici, 1544 erbaut, seit 1803 Sitz der Französischen Akademie

Views of St. Peter's:
St Pierre vue:
Ansichten von St. Peter:

from Via della Conciliazione
de la Via della Conciliazione
von der Via della Conciliazione

from a bank of the Tiber
d'une rive du Tibre
vom Tiberufer

St. Peter's Square and the Church of St. Peter. The building was begun in 1506 and consecrated in 1626. It was designed by Bramante and Michelangelo (with façade by Carlo Maderna), and the beautiful colonnades in the square are the work of Bernini

La place et la basilique St Pierre. L'édifice, entrepris en 1506, fut consacré en 1626. Il fut construit d'après les plans de Bramante et de Michel-Ange (façade de Carlo Maderna) et les belles colonnades de la place sont l'oeuvre du Bernin

Petersplatz und Peterskirche; 1506 wurde mit dem Neubau begonnen, 1626 wurde er geweiht. Die Pläne des Zentralbaus stammen im wesentlichen von Bramante und Michelangelo, Langhaus und Vorhalle von Carlo Maderna, die schönen Säulengänge des Petersplatzes von Bernini

43

Colonnades at the right-hand entrance to St. Peter's Square
Colonnades à droite de l'entrée de la place St Pierre
Rechter Flügel der Säulenhallen am Eingang des Petersplatzes

The fountains of Rome—like this one by Maderna in St. Peter's Square—are an enchanting feature of the city, and they are loved as much for their beautiful designs . . .

Les fontaines de Rome, telle que celle de Maderna, place St Pierre, sont de ravissants ornements de la ville et sont aimées autant pour leurs belles formes . . .

Die Brunnen Roms — dieser hier von Maderna auf dem Petersplatz — sind ein bezauberndes Merkmal der Stadt; ihr Reiz liegt ebenso sehr in den schönen Entwürfen . . .

. . . as for the cool relief they provide from the sometimes oppressive weight of the city's monuments. Above: the Neptune fountain in the Piazza Navona

. . . que pour le contraste qu'elles offrent avec la massivité parfois pesante des monuments de la ville. Ci-dessus la fontaine Neptune sur la Piazza Navona

. . . wie in dem kühlen Abstand, den sie von den zuweilen erdrückenden Bauwerken der Stadt wahren. Neptun-Brunnen auf der Piazza Navona

Water from an ogre's mouth: fountain in the Piazza della Rotonda
De la bouche d'un ogre: fontaine de la Piazza della Rotonda
Wasser aus dem Mund eines Ogers: Brunnen auf der Piazza della Rotonda

Water from a lion's mouth: fountain in
the Piazza del Popolo

De la bouche d'un lion : fontaine de la
Piazza del Popolo

Wasser aus dem Rachen eines Löwen:
Brunnen auf der Piazza del Popolo

If you are about to leave Rome, and throw a coin into the Fontana di Trevi, you won't have looked on the city for the last time
Selon la légende, quiconque, avant de quitter Rome, jette une pièce de monnaie dans la fontaine de Trevi est sûr d'y revenir
Die Überlieferung sagt, wer beim Abschied eine Münze in die Fontana di Trevi werfe, der werde Rom wiedersehen

Fountains at the Villa d'Este, Tivoli, which is one of the most delightful spots to be visited in the immediate vicinity of Rome
Les fontaines de la villa d'Este à Tivoli, l'un des plus délicieux endroits des environs de Rome
Brunnen an der Villa d'Este in Tivoli, eine der reizvollsten Sehenswürdigkeiten in der Umgebung Roms

Fountain of the Triton, designed by Bernini, in the Piazza Barberini
La fontaine du Triton, conçue par le Bernin, place Barberini
Triton-Brunnen auf der Piazza Barberini, Entwurf von Bernini

The piazze of Rome are adorned by obelisks as well as fountains: they were imported from Egypt in ancient times. Obelisk in the Piazza della Minerva, from the temple of Isis

Les places de Rome sont ornées d'obélisques aussi bien que de fontaines : ceux-ci furent autrefois rapportés d'Egypte. L'obélisque de la Piazza della Minerva provient du temple d'Isis

Gleich den Brunnen schmücken Obelisken die Plätze Roms: sie wurden in alten Zeiten aus Ägypten hierher verpflanzt. Obelisk auf der Piazza della Minerva, einstmals am Tempel der Isis

51

The church of S. Agnese in Agone and the Fontana dei Fiumi. The obelisk on the right is a Roman imitation

L'église Ste Agnes d'Agon et la fontaine dei Fiumi. L'obélisque que l'on voit à droite est une imitation romaine.

Die Kirche S. Agnese in Agone und die Fontana dei Fiumi.
Der Obelisk rechts ist eine römische Nachbildung

Obelisk in the Piazza di S. Giovanni in Laterano which is the oldest of Rome's obelisks: it dates back nearly 3500 years

L'obélisque de la place St Jean de Latran, le plus ancien des obélisques de Rome, remonte à près à 3.500 ans

Der älteste Obelisk Roms, auf der Piazza di S. Giovanni in Laterano: er ist etwa 3500 Jahre alt

Obelisk in St. Peter's Square, from the Circus of Nero. The only obelisk in Rome without hieroglyphics

L'obélisque de la place St Pierre, provenant du cirque de Néron, le seul de Rome qui ne porte pas d'hiéroglyphes

Obelisk auf dem Petersplatz, früher im Circus des Nero; der einzige Obelisk Roms, der keine Hieroglyphen trägt

This obelisk in the Piazza del Popolo is the second oldest in Rome: it was brought to Rome from Heliopolis by Augustus, after the conquest of Egypt

Cet obélisque de la Piazza del Popolo est l'un des plus anciens de Rome: il fut rapporté d'Héliopolis par Auguste, après la conquête de l'Egypte

Dieser Obelisk auf der Piazza del Popolo ist der zweitälteste Roms: nach der Eroberung Ägyptens brachte ihn Augustus aus Heliopolis mit

View along the Via del Corso from the Victor Emmanuel II monument
Le monument à Victor-Emmanuel II vu de la Via del Corso
Blick vom Denkmal Viktor Emmanuels II. in die Via del Corso

The Colosseum, or Flavian Amphitheatre, was the largest of Roman amphitheatres. The building, begun by Vespasian and completed in A.D. 80, could hold about 50,000 spectators. According to tradition, many Christians suffered martyrdom here

Le Colisée, ou amphithéâtre Flavien, était le plus grand des amphithéâtres romains. L'édifice, entrepris sous Vespasien et achevé en 80 de notre ère, pouvait recevoir 50.000 spectateurs. Suivant la tradition, de nombreux chrétiens y furent martyrisés

Das Kolosseum, auch flavisches Amphitheater genannt, war das größte der römischen Amphitheater. Der Bau, von Vespasian begonnen und im Jahr 80 n. Chr. vollendet, faßte rund 50 000 Zuschauer. Nach der Überlieferung erlitten hier zahlreiche Christen den Märtyrertod

Another view of the Colosseum
Une autre vue du Colisée
Teilansicht des Kolosseums

A view of the Colosseum arena, which was used for gladiatoria l
combats and other spectacles

Vue de l'arène du Colisée, où se déroulaient des combats de
gladiateurs et d'autres spectacles

Ein Blick in die Arena des Kolosseums, die Gladiatoren-
kämpfen und anderen Schauspielen diente

The afterglow of 'the splendour that was Rome' lingers in ruins such as these: the Theatre of Marcellus, begun by Julius Caesar and completed in 13 B.C.

Un dernier reflet de «la splendeur que fut Rome» subsiste dans des ruines telles que celles-ci: le théâtre de Marcellus, commencé sous Jules César et achevé en l'an 13 av. J.C.

Der Nachglanz Roms nistet in solchen Ruinen: das Marcellus-Theater, von Julius Caesar begonnen, 13 v. Chr. vollendet

Angel designed by Bernini, on the Bridge of S. Angelo. The vivid Baroque aspect of the city owes much to the genius of Bernini, whose style is marked by a florid inventiveness

Un ange du Bernin, sur le point Saint-Ange. Le vivant aspect baroque de la cité doit beaucoup au génie du Bernin, dont le style est marqué d'une imagination débordante

Engelsstatue von Bernini, auf der Engelsbrücke. Viel von ihrem lebendigen Barockcharakter verdankt die Stadt dem Geist und der unermüdlichen Schöpferkraft Berninis

Looking across the Forum Romanum, a focal point of life in ancient Rome. The Temple of Antoninus and Faustina is seen in centre, remains of the Arch of Augustus in left foreground

Le Forum Romanum, l'un des principaux centres de la vie romaine dans l'Antiquité. Le temple d'Antonin et Faustine est au centre; au premier plan à gauche, les restes de l'arc de triomphe d'Auguste

Blick auf das Forum Romanum, einen Brennpunkt des öffentlichen Lebens im alten Rom. In der Mitte der Tempel von Antoninus und Faustina, links im Vordergrund Reste des Augustus-Bogens

Part of the Arch of Septimius Severus in the Forum Romanum
Une partie de l'arc de triomphe de Septime Sévère sur le Forum Romanum
Ein Teil des Severus-Bogens im Forum Romanum

Part of Trajan's Forum (left foreground), showing the semicircular market hall of Trajan. The forum is
thought to be the work of the architect Apollodorus of Damascus
Une partie du Forum Trajan (au premier plan, à droite), où l'on voit le marché semi-circulaire de Trajan.
Ce forum serait l'œuvre de l'architecte Apollodore de Damas
Teile des Trajans-Forums (links im Vordergrund) mit der halbrunden Markthalle des Trajan. Das Forum
gilt als das Werk des Architekten Apollodoros von Damaskus

The Forum Romanum and SS. Martina e Luca. Left of the baroque-fronted church is the Temple of Vespasian, on the right the Arch of Septimius Severus and the Temple of Saturn

Le Forum Romanum et l'église St Martin et St Luc. A gauche de l'église baroque, on voit le temple de Vespasien, à droite l'arc de Septime Sévère et le temple de Saturne

Forum Romanum und SS. Martina e Luca. Links von der Kirche mit ihrer Barockfassade der Tempel des Vespasian, rechts der Severus-Bogen und der Tempel des Saturn

Part of the Forum Romanum, showing three columns of the Temple of Vespasian and eight of the Temple of Saturn
Une partie du Forum Romanum; on reconnaît trois colonnes du temple de Vespasien et huit du temple de Saturne
Teilansicht vom Forum Romanum: drei Säulen vom Tempel des Vespasian und acht vom Tempel des Saturn

Columns of the Temple of Castor and Pollux and ruins of the Basilica
Julia, with SS. Martina e Luca in background
Colonnes du temple de Castor et Pollux et ruines de la basilique
Julia, avec l'église St Martin et St Luc à l'arrière-plan
Säulen des Tempels der Dioskuren Castor and Pollux und Reste der
Basilica Julia. Im Hintergrund SS. Martina e Luca

Columns, ancient and modern
Colonnes, anciennes et modernes
Säulen: antik — und modern

The famous church of S. Maria in Cosmedin, with part of the so-called Temple of Vesta in foreground
La fameuse église Ste Marie en Cosmedin; au premier plan une partie du temple de Vesta
Die berühmte Kirche S. Maria in Cosmedin, im Vordergrund ein Stück vom sogenannten Tempel der Vesta

Young Romans at play under the Arch of Janus Quadrifons, with the 'Temple of Vesta' in background
Jeunes Romains jouant sous l'arc de Janus Quadrifons, avec le temple de Vesta à l'arrière-plan
Römische Jungen beim Spiel unter dem Bogen des Janus Quadrifons, im Hintergrund der „Tempel der Vesta"

The Arch of Titus was dedicated by Domitian to commemorate a series of victories which ended in the sack of Jerusalem, and reconstructed for Pius VII

L'arc de triomphe de Titus, érigé par Domitien pour commémorer une série de victoires qui mirent fin au sac de Jérusalem, fut reconstruit pour Pie VII

Titus-Bogen, erbaut von Domitian zur Erinnerung an eine Reihe von Siegen, die mit der Zerstörung Jerusalems endeten; für Pius VII. wiedererrichtet

The Arch of Constantine, erected in the fourth century A.D. by the Senate and people of Rome in honour of
Constantine's victory over Maxentius

L'arc de triomphe de Constantin, construit au IVème siècle par le Sénat et le peuple de Rome en l'honneur de la
victoire de Constantin sur Maxence

Der Konstantins-Bogen, im 4. Jahrhundert n. Chr. von Senat und Volk von Rom errichtet zu Ehren von Konstantins
Sieg über Maxentius

Capitoline Square, with the famous equestrian statue of Marcus Aurelius
La place du Capitole, avec la fameuse statue équestre de Marc-Aurèle
Die berühmte Reiterstatue des Mark Aurel auf dem Kapitol

The Palazzo dei Senatori
on the Capitol. The buil-
ding was designed by
Michelangelo

Le palais des Sénateurs
sur le Capitole. Edifice
construit par Michel-
Ange

Der Palazzo dei Senatori
auf dem Kapitol, Ent-
wurf von Michelangelo

Point of view: at the top of the Capitol steps
Panorama: en haut des escaliers du Capitole
Aussichten: auf der Höhe der Stufen zum Kapitol

The two colossal statues of the Discori above the Capitol steps
Les deux statues colossales des Discori dominant les escaliers du Capitole
Die beiden Kolossalstatuen der Dioskuren über den Stufen zum Kapitol

Up and down the Capitol steps
Sur les escaliers du Capitole
Auf und ab auf den Stufen zum Kapitol

The so-called Temple of Fortuna Virilis, a notable example of Graeco-Italic architecture
Le temple de la Fortune virile, remarquable exemple d'architecture gréco-romaine
Der sogenannte Tempel der Fortuna Virilis, ein bemerkenswertes Beispiel griechisch-italienischer Architektur

77

Ornamental urns and statuary in the picturesque 17th century gardens behind the Galleria Borghese
Urnes et statues ornementales dans les pittoresques jardins du XVIIème siècle qui bordent la galerie Borghèse
Ziergefäße und Statuen in den malerischen Gärten hinter der Galleria Borghese, einer Anlage im Stil des 17. Jahrhunderts

The charming artificial lake in the Villa Borghese, with the modern Temple of Aesculapius in view across the water
Le charmant lac artificiel de la villa Borghèse, avec le temple moderne d'Esculape dans le lointain
Der bezaubernde künstliche Teich der Villa Borghese, im Blickfeld jenseits des Wassers der moderne Tempel des Äskulap

A touch of Egypt: the pyramid of Caius Cestius, in the grounds of the famous Protestant cemetery where Shelley and Keats lie buried

Evocation de l'Egypte : la pyramide de Caius Cestius, dans le fameux cimetière protestant où sont enterrés Shelley et Keats

Ein Hauch Ägyptens: die Pyramide des Caius Cestius. Daneben liegt der berühmte Friedhof der Nichtkatholiken, auf dem Shelley und Keats begraben sind

Detail of the Casino of Pius IV in the Vatican gardens, which was built in the mid-sixteenth century
Détail du «Casino» de Pie IV dans les jardins du Vatican, construit au milieu du XVIème siècle
Detail des Casino di Pio IV in den päpstlichen Gärten, Mitte des 16. Jahrhunderts erbaut

Entrance to the Vatican Museums, which house superb collections of the art of antiquity
L'Entrée du musée du Vatican, qui renferme de superbes collections d'art antique
Eingang der Vatikanischen Museen, die prachtvolle Sammlungen antiker Kunst enthalten

The Porta Pia, erected in the sixteenth century, stands at the end of the Via Venti Settembre
La Porta Pia, érigée au XVIème siècle, s'élève à l'extrémité de la Via Venti Settembre
Die Porta Pia, erbaut im 16. Jahrhundert, am Ende der Via Venti Settembre

Two views of Trajan's column. This column was raised to Emperor Trajan in the second century A.D.: it is covered with a spiral band of reliefs which represent Trajan's two campaigns in Dacia

Deux vues de la colonne trajane. Cette colonne fut élevée à l'empereur Trajan au deuxième siècle ap. J. C.; elle est recouverte d'une spirale de bas-reliefs représentants les deux campagnes de l'empereur en Dacie

Zwei Ansichten der Trajans-Säule. Sie wurde im 2. Jahrhundert n. Chr. zu Ehren des Kaisers Trajan errichtet und zeigt auf spiralförmigen Reliefbändern die beiden Feldzüge Trajans gegen Dacien

85

Left, the church of S. Maria di Loreto, and behind Trajan's column the church of SS. Nome di Maria

L'église Ste Marie di Loreto (à gauche) et derrière la colonne trajane, l'église SS. Nome di Maria

Links die Kirche S. Maria di Loreto, hinter der Trajans-Säule SS. Nome di Maria

Trajan's column and the church of SS. Nome di Maria

La colonne trajane di l'église SS. Nome et Maria

Trajans-Säule und die Kirche SS. Nome di Maria

87

View of the Forum Romanum
Vue du Forum Romanum
Ansicht des Forum Romanum

Statues on the roof of St. Peter's
Statues sur le toit de la basilique St Pierre
Statuen auf dem Dach von St. Peter

Colossal statues of athletes surrounding
the Marble Stadium in the Campo della
Farnesina

Statues colossales d'athlètes entourant le
stade de marbre sur le Campo della Farnesina

Kolossalstatuen von Athleten umsäumen
das Marmorstadion im Campo della Farnesina

One of the seven hills of the Eternal City, the Palatine: here some of the most ancient relics of the city are to be seen
Le Palatin, une des sept collines de Rome: l'on y voit quelques-unes des plus anciennes reliques de la ville
Der Palatin, einer der sieben Hügel der Ewigen Stadt: hier findet man einige der ältesten Überbleibsel des einstigen Rom

Porta Maggiore, which consists of two aqueducts built by the Emperor Claudius in the first century A.D.
La porte Majeure, composée de deux acqueducs construits par l'empereur Claude au premier siècle ap. J.C.
Die Porta Maggiore, ein doppelter Aquädukt, erbaut von Kaiser Claudius im I. Jahrhundert n. Chr.

Porta S. Sebastiano, ancient gateway set in the Aurelian Wall
La porte St Sébestien, ancienne trouée dans l'enceinte aurélienne
Die Porta S. Sebastiano, ein altes Stadttor in der Aurelianischen Mauer

Ruins of the Basilica of Constantine seen from the House of the Vestal Virgins, who were guardians of Vesta's sacred fire
Les ruines de la basilique de Constantin vues de la maison des Vestales, gardiennes du feu sacré
Die Ruinen der Konstantins-Basilika; Blick aus dem Atrium Vestae, dem Gebäude der Vestalischen Jungfrauen, der Hüterinnen des heiligen
Feuers der Vesta

On the steps leading from Via Cavour to S. Pietro in Vincoli
Sur les escaliers menant de la Via Cavour à St Pierre-ès-liens
Auf den Stufen von der Via Cavour zur Kirche S. Pietro in Vincoli

94

The history of the Basilica of S. Giovanni in Laterano dates back to Constantine. It is the cathedral church of the Bishop of Rome. (Left) the basilica, and (below) the statue of St. Francis of Assisi with the basilica in background

L'histoire de la Basilique St Jean de Latran remonte à Constantin. C'est la cathédrale de l'évêque de Rome. (A gauche) la basilique, (au-dessous) la statue de St François d'Assise, avec la basilique à l'arrière-plan

Die Geschichte der Basilika S. Giovanni in Laterano geht zurück auf Konstantin; sie ist die Bischofskirche des Papstes. — Links: die Basilika, rechts: Statue des heiligen Franz von Assisi mit der Basilika im Hintergrund

The church of S. Paolo fuori le Mura (St. Paul without the walls), dedicated A.D. 386: this church, the largest in Rome after St. Peter's, was under the protection of the Kings of England until the Reformation

L'église St Paul-hors-les-murs, consacrée en 386; cette église, la plus grande de Rome après St Pierre, fut sous la protection des rois d'Angleterre jusqu'à la Réforme

Die Kirche S. Paolo fuori le Mura (St. Paul vor den Mauern), 386 n. Chr. geweiht, ist nach St. Peter die größte Kirche Roms. Bis zur Reformation stand sie unter der Schutzherrschaft der englischen Könige

The church of SS. Giovanni e Paolo, dedicated to two saints who suffered martyrdom in the fourth century
L'église Sts Jean et Paul, consacrée aux deux saints martyrisés au IVème siècle
Die Kirche SS. Giovanni e Paolo, den beiden Heiligen geweiht, die im 4. Jahrhundert n. Chr. den Märtyrertod erlitten

Courtyard of S. Paolo fuori le Mura, showing part of the façade of the basilica
Cour de St Paul-hors-les-murs d'où l'on voit une partie de la façade de la basilique
Vorhof der Kirche S. Paolo fuori le Mura mit Teilansicht der Fassade der Basilika

The church of S. Maria in Trastevere, which was the first Roman church to be dedicated to the Virgin Mary
L'église Ste Marie en Trastevere, la première église romaine consacrée à la Vierge Marie
S. Maria in Trastevere, die erste römische Kirche, die der Jungfrau Maria geweiht wurde

S. Maria in Aracoeli, near which Gibbon conceived the idea of writing his history of the Decline and Fall of Rome
L'église Sainte Marie in Aracoeli, près de laquelle Gibbon conçut le projet d'écrire son livre «Décadence et chute de l'empire romain»
Die Kirche S. Maria in Aracoeli, in deren Nähe Gibbon den Plan faßte, seine Geschichte des Verfalls und Untergangs des römischen Reiches zu schreiben

S. Croce in Gerusalemme, said to have been founded by Constantine to enshrine the relics of the True Cross, found by his mother in Jerusalem
Sainte Croix de Jérusalem, qui aurait été fondée par Constantin pour recevoir les reliques de la Vraie Croix, que sa mère recueillit à Jérusalem
Die Kirche S. Croce in Gerusalemme, der Überlieferung nach von Konstantin begründet als Aufbewahrungsstätte der Reliquien vom
Heiligen Kreuz, die seine Mutter in Jerusalem gefunden hatte

The Vatican Picture Gallery, built
in 1932 by Pius XI: the gallery
contains a magnificent collection
of religious art

Le musée de peinture du Vatican,
achevé en 1932 par Pie XI, renferme une magnifique collection
d'art religieux

Die Pinakothek des Vatikan, 1932
von Pius XI. erbaut: Die Galerie
enthält eine prachtvolle Sammlung
religiöser Kunst

Ancient city walls at Porta S. Sebastiano

Mur de l'ancienne enceinte, porte Saint Sébastien

Alte Stadtmauer an der Porta S. Sebastiano

The church of S. Gregorio Magno, which was originally built by St. Gregory the Great, and later restored

L'église St Grégoire le Grand, construite par St Grégoire lui-même, ultérieurement restaurée

Die Kirche S. Gregorio Magno, ursprünglich erbaut von Gregor dem Großen, später restauriert

Part of Porta S. Sebastiano

Une partie de la porte St
Sébastien

Teilansicht der Porta S. Sebastiano

The Appian Way, most famous of the roads that led to Rome: it was begun in 312 B.C., and the road and its ruined monuments ar still extant

La Voie Appienne, la plus célèbre des routes vers Rome: entreprise en 312 av. J.C., elle existe encore de nos jours avec les restes de quelques-uns de ses monuments

Die Via Appia, die berühmteste der Straßen nach Rom: 312 v. Chr. wurde mit dem Bau begonnen, und sowohl die Straße wie die Ruine ihrer Bauten sind noch heute vorhanden

Along the Appian Way: ruins of a church (left), the Tomb
of Caecilia Metella (right)

Le long de la Voie Appienne: ruines d'une église (à
gauche), tombe de Caecilia Metella (à droite)

An der Via Appia, links die Ruinen einer Kirche, rechts
das Grabmal der Caecilia Metella

Wall of Aurelian
Enceinte d'Aurélien
Die Aurelianische Stadtmauer

Cats and capitals: among the ruins of the Colosseum
Chats et chapiteaux: parmi les ruines du Colisée
Katzen und Kapitelle: in den Ruinen des Kolosseums

Mosaic floor of the Baths of Caracalla one of the ancient Roman 'thermae'
Mosaïque des Thermes de Caracalla, l'un des plus anciens de Rome
Mosaikboden der Thermen des Caracalla

Youth and antiquity: walking in the ruined Theatre of Marcellus
Jeunes gens dans le théâtre en ruines de Marcellus
Jugend und Antike: ein Gang durch die Ruinen des Marcellus-Theaters

Relaxing under the colonnades in St. Peter's Square
Farniente sous les colonnades de la place St Pierre
Ruhepause unter den Kolonnaden des Petersplatzes

Light streams in through the top of St. Peter's dome: in silhouette below is part of the massive baldacchino by Bernini which stands above the Papal altar

Rayons de lumière filtrant à travers le dôme de St Pierre; à l'arrière-plan se silhouette une partie du massif baldaquin du Bernin qui s'élève au-dessus de l'autel pontifical

Helles Licht strömt ein durch die „Laterne" der Peterskuppel. Darunter in der Silhouette ein Teil des steinernen Baldachins von Bernini über dem Hochaltar

Detail of the dome of St. Peter's
Détail du dôme de St Pierre
Teilansicht der Kuppel von St. Peter

Cappella del Coro in St. Peter's
Chappelle del Coro à St Pierre
Chorkapelle im Petersdom

Statue of St. Peter in St. Peter's, which is probably the work of Arnolfo di Cambio

Statue de St Pierre à St Pierre de Rome, attribuée à Arnolfo di Cambio

Statue des heiligen Petrus im Petersdom, wahrscheinlich ein Werk von Arnolfo di Cambio

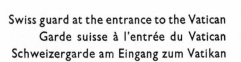

Swiss guard at the entrance to the Vatican
Garde suisse à l'entrée du Vatican
Schweizergarde am Eingang zum Vatikan

Inside the church of the SS. Apostoli, which has its origins in the sixth century A.D.
Intérieur de l'église des Saints Apôtres, qui remonte au VIème siècle
Innenraum der Kirche SS. Apostoli, deren Ursprung im 6. Jahrhundert n. Chr. liegt

The church of S. Vitale, interior
Intérieur de l'église S. Vitale
Altarraum der Kirche S. Vitale

S. Paolo fuori le Mura: a view of the cloister
St Paul-hors-les-murs : vue du cloître
S. Paolo fuori le Mura, Kreuzgang

Michelangelo's celebrated statue of Moses in the church of S. Pietro in Vincoli
La célèbre statue de Moïse, de Michel-Ange, à l'église St Pierre-ès-liens
Michelangelos gefeierte Moses-Statue in der Kirche S. Pietro in Vincoli

Rome honours its great men: the equestrian statue of Victor Emmanuel II, which stands 37 feet high
Rome honore ses grands hommes: statue équestre de Victor-Emmanuel II, haute de plus de dix mètres
Rom ehrt seine großen Männer: die rund 11 m hohe Reiterstatue Viktor Emmanuels II.

Equestrian statue of Garibaldi, maker of modern Italy: on the Janiculum Promenade

Statue équestre de Garibaldi, constructeur de l'Italie moderne, sur la promenade du Janicule

Reiterstatue Garibaldis, des Schöpfers des modernen Staates Italien, auf der Passeggiata del Gianicolo

Statue of Lord Byron, one of the many northerners of genius who have found inspiration in Rome

Statue de Lord Byron, l'un des nombreux génies du Nord qui trouvèrent l'inspiration à Rome

Statue Lord Byrons, eines der vielen genialen Nordländer, die in Rom neue Inspiration gefunden haben

Statue of the Persian poet Firdousi, presented to Rome by the citizens of Teheran

Statue du poète persan Firdousi, offerte à Rome par les habitants de Téhéran

Statue des persischen Dichters Firdausi, eine Gabe der Bürger Teherans an die Stadt Rom

Lighthouse on the Janiculum
Promenade, presented to
Rome by Italian settlers in
the Argentine

Phare de la promenade du Janicule, offert à Rome par une
colonie d'Italiens émigrés en
Argentine

Leuchtturm auf der Passeggiata
del Gianicolo, der Stadt Rom
von italienischen Siedlern in
Argentinien gestiftet

View from the Janiculum Promenade
Vue prise de la promenade du Janicule
Blick von der Passeggiata del Gianicolo

View over Rome from Pincio Hill
Rome vue de la colline du Pincio
Blick vom Monte Pincio auf Rom

126

Palm trees in the garden of the
Piazza Cairoli, the fine Baroque
church of S. Carlo ai Catinari
in background

Palmiers du jardin de la Piazza
Cairoli; l'arrière-plan la belle
église baroque de S. Carlo ai
Catinari

Palmen in den Grünanlagen
der Piazza Cairoli, im Hintergrund die schöne Barockkirche
S. Carlo ai Catinari

Vatican gardens, showing part of the Sistine chapel on right

Les jardins du Vatican, avec une partie de la chapelle Sixtine
à droite

Die päpstlichen Gärten, rechts ein Teil der Sixtinischen
Kapelle

View of the Galleria Borghese, home of an important art
collection

Vue de la Galerie Borghèse, où se trouve une importante
collection d'art

Die Galleria Borghese, Sitz einer bedeutenden Kunst-
sammlung

Life flows quietly through the back streets of the city, away from the sights

La vie s'écoule doucement dans les petites rues du bas de la ville, loin des merveilles de la cité

In den abgelegenen Straßen, fern von den Sehenswürdigkeiten, fließt das Leben ruhiger

Thoroughfare
Une place animée
Durchgangsverkehr

On the sunny side of the street
Un coin ensoleillé
Auf der Sonnenseite des Lebens?

For favours received: religious thanksgiving plaques cover a wall in the Piazzale Brasile
Une multitude d'ex-votos recouvre un mur de la Piazzale Brasile
Zum Dank für erwiesene Gnaden: Votivtafeln an einer Wand des Piazzale Brasile

The shadows lengthen
Les ombres s'allongent
Die Schatten werden länger

Scene in the Trastevere quarter
Une scène dans le quartier du Trastevere
Im Stadtviertel Trastevere

Life in a small piazza
Instantané sur une petite place
Das Leben auf einem kleinen Platz

Rome moves with the times: a modern hospital in the Via Amba Aradam

Rome marche avec son temps: hôpital moderne, Via Amba Aradam

Rom geht mit der Zeit: modernes Krankenhaus in der Via Amba Aradam

Station Termini at night
Stazione Termini, la nuit
Bahnhof Termini bei Nacht

A modern bridge crosses the Tiber

Un pont moderne enjambe le Tibre

Moderne Brücke über den Tiber

The Ponte Fabricio is the oldest extant bridge in Rome, dating back to 64 B.C.

Le pont Fabricio est le plus ancien de Rome. Il remonte à 64 av. J.C.

Der Ponte Fabricio aus dem Jahr 64 v. Chr. ist die älteste erhaltene Brücke Roms

Island of the Tiber, which was once sacred to the god Aesculapius

L'île du Tibre, autrefois consacrée au dieu Esculape

Tiberinsel, einst dem Gott Äskulap geweiht

A river of history: empires decline and fall, but the Tiber flows forever
Un fleuve chargé d'histoire: les empires déclinent et tombent, le Tibre coule toujours
Ein geschichtsträchtiger Fluß: Kaiserreiche sind vergangen, der Tiber bleibt

ROME AT LEISURE

Rome en Flânant   **Rom in seiner Freizeit**

Boats on the Tiber
Embarcations sur le Tibre
Boote auf dem Tiber

A place for Roman Holidays: Ostia beach at high tide
Vacances romaines : la plage d'Ostie à marée haute
Rom in Ferien: der Strand von Ostia bei Flut

City lights
Les lumières de la ville
Lichter der Großstadt

Evening rush hour
La foule à la sortie des bureau
Abendlicher Berufsverkehr

Rome illuminated: (above and below) the Forum Romanum, and
(right) the Fountain of the Republic

Rome illuminée : (ci-dessus et ci-dessous) le Forum et (à droite) la
• Fontaine de la République

Rom in Scheinwerferlicht: das Forum Romanum (Bild oben und
unten) und die Fontana della Repubblica

A goddess . . .
Une déesse . . .
Eine Gottheit . . .

... has an admirer
... a un admirateur
... findet ihren Bewunderer

The modern woman, too . . .
La femme moderne aussi . . .
Auch die Frau von heute . . .

148

...has her admirers
...a ses admirateurs
...hat ihre Bewunderer

Catch me if you can!
Coucou!
Fang mich doch!

Playing is a serious business
Le jeu est une affaire sérieuse
Spielen ist eine ernsthafte Angelegenheit

Ordering ices
Devant le marchand de glaces
Großbestellung auf Eis

Boy alone . . .
Un garçon seul . . .
Ein Junge allein . . .

. . . boys together: 'Why photograph us?'

. . . Plusieurs garçons ensemble: «Pourquoi nous photographier?»

. . . ein paar beisammen: Warum will er uns wohl photographieren?

Important occasions: a first communion . . .
Grand événements : première communion . . .
Wichtige Ereignisse: Erstkommunion . . .

. . . a fashionable wedding
. . . mariage élégant
. . . eine elegante Hochzeit

What people do to amuse themselves ...
Ce que font les gens pour se distraire ...
Womit sich manche Leute die Zeit vertreiben ...

... is sometimes a mystery ...
... est parfois un mystère ...
... bleibt zuweilen ein Geheimnis ...

... to those who watch them
... pour ceux qui les observent
... für den Beobachter

155

Moments of decision: 'Shall I try my luck?'
Moments de décision: «Tenter la chance?»
Augenblicke der Entscheidung: Soll ich mein Glück versuchen?

'Shall we have our picture taken?'
«Nous ferons-nous photographier?»
„Wollen wir uns photographieren lassen?"

The patience of statues . . .
La patience des statues . . .
Statuen sind geduldig . . .

     . . . with the look of being looked at
     . . . qui doivent se savoir regardées
     . . . und gewohnt, angestarrt zu werden

Venus truncated
Vénus tronquée
Verstümmelte Venus

Movement arrested
Mouvement interrompu
Steingewordene Bewegung

'Do you come here often?'
«Est-ce que vous venez ici souvent?»
„Sind Sie öfter hier?"

Rome observed: evening
Evocation de Rome : Image nocturne
Wächter über der Stadt: Rom am Abend